...nd Information Service
...ov.uk/libraries
...4 661511

KT-429-463

THE WORLD OF
EXPLORATION

Philip Wilkinson

KINGFISHER

A L I S

1722238

KINGFISHER

Kingfisher Publications Plc
New Penderel House,
283–288 High Holborn,
London WC1V 7HZ
www.kingfisherpub.com

ABERDEENSHIRE LIBRARY AND	
INFORMATION SERVICES	
1722238	
HJ	433330
J910.9	£5.99
JU	JNF

First published by Kingfisher Publications Plc 2006
10 9 8 7 6 5 4 3 2 1

1TR/1105/TIMS/PICA(PICA)/128MA/F

Copyright © Kingfisher Publications Plc 2006

First published in 2002 as *The Best-Ever Book of Exploration*

All rights reserved. No part of this publication may be
reproduced, stored in a retrieval system or transmitted by
any means, electronic, mechanical, photocopying or
otherwise, without prior permission of the publisher.

A CIP catalogue record for this book is available from
the British Library.

ISBN-13: 978 0 7534 1344 9
ISBN-10: 0 7534 1344 2

Editor: Carron Brown
Senior designer: Jane Tassie
Cover designer: Heidi Appleton
Consultant: Shane Winser,
    The Royal Geographical Society, London
Production controller: Debbie Otter
DTP manager: Nicky Studdart
Picture research manager: Jane Lambert
Picture research assistant: Rachael Swann
Artwork archivists: Wendy Allison and Steve Robinson

Printed in China

The Publisher would like to thank the **Royal
Geographical Society (with The Institute of British
Geographers)** for their help and co-operation
in the production of this book.

Since its formation in 1830, the Royal Geographical
Society has sponsored and supported expeditions
and fieldwork throughout the world. Today it is
at the forefront of geographical research and
education. The Society's Expedition Advisory
Centre provides information, training and advice
to hundreds of expeditions and field research
projects each year.

Further information about the Society can be
obtained from its website: www.rgs.org

CONTENTS

BEING AN EXPLORER

People have been travelling into the unknown in search of new knowledge for centuries – these men and women are called explorers. Early explorers travelled for all sorts of different reasons – to find new places to farm and settle, to claim lands for their rulers, to spread religions or to make money. It was often dangerous work. They set off to places that had not been mapped, where the weather was unpredictable and where they might encounter hostile peoples. Modern explorers are most likely to travel for scientific reasons, to better understand the world we live in. They can call on improved technology, but they need to be just as resourceful as their ancestors. The biggest physical challenges are in the most remote areas of the world – the polar ice caps, the deepest oceans and even space – where explorers need to be well-prepared, properly equipped and brave.

Well-equipped
Expeditions can take years to plan. Explorers have to raise money, gather together a team of people, and find the right equipment. A major expedition might require a huge amount of equipment, from vehicles and tents to medical supplies, fuel, food, clothing and the items needed for research to be carried out. Everything has to be chosen with care, and tested before the expedition sets off.

Stranded!

Whatever the reason for exploration, going where no one has gone before requires commitment and resourcefulness. In the past, a polar explorer did not even have a radio to summon help if he was stranded – he could use only what he had with him and what he could find to help him survive. But even with today's hi-tech equipment, explorers still need these qualities when they venture into new environments.

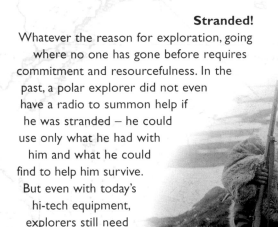

Fire-lighting

Making fire has always been one of the most important survival skills. Fire gives us warmth and provides heat for cooking. A modern explorer might carry several aids to start a fire – waterproof matches, a flint and steel to make sparks, and a magnifying glass to focus the sun's powerful rays on one spot, heating it until it is so hot that it burns.

Could you be an explorer?

To be an explorer you need to feel at home in the outdoors and, in due course, learn skills such as map-reading, setting up and living in a camp, and first aid. The easiest way to start is to take part in properly organized outdoor activities through your school or youth club. As you do so, you will begin to realize that there are many qualities you need to play a part in a successful expedition. You will need to be able to plan, research, and be a good team player. But if you can do these things, finding and sharing new knowledge is one of the most rewarding of human activities. When you are ready to venture further, you will find many organizations are willing to give advice. In Britain, for example, the Royal Geographical Society (with The Institute of British Geographers) has an Expedition Advisory Centre that can put you in touch with groups organizing overseas expeditions for young people.

Preparation and survival

Explorers travel through unknown and often difficult terrain. They can face many different dangers, and help may be far away. To survive harsh conditions, explorers have to be prepared and equipped for survival. The expedition leader needs to pick a balanced team with a range of abilities and experience within the group, such as medical skills and experience of the terrain. To have the best chance of success, each team member needs to do plenty of research to find out all they can about the conditions they are likely to encounter.

Climbing towards the canopy
Jungle trees grow tall, their branches and leaves forming a high, dense layer called the canopy. This is where much of the rainforest wildlife lives, and plants flower and fruit. To study the canopy, explorers climb the trees using ropes, aluminium ladders and the knowledge of local climbers.

In the wet
Rainforests are the most humid places on the earth, so the jungle traveller has to get used to being wet most of the time. But jungle travellers do not usually wear waterproof clothing – it tends to keep in the heat, and just makes the wearer sweaty and uncomfortable. Tough, lightweight clothes that can be washed and dried quickly are best in this sort of environment.

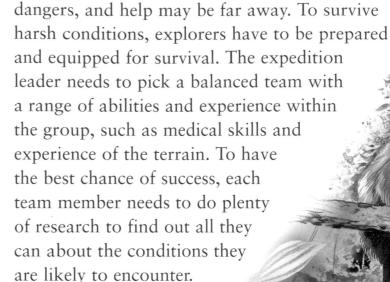

Measuring up
These scientists are surveying an area of cleared rainforest in Brazil. The plants are growing back to form dense secondary jungle. This thick forest vegetation is very difficult to travel through and explore.

In the rainforest

Tropical rainforest is a challenging environment for explorers. It is hot, sticky, dark and noisy. The thick vegetation blocks out a lot of light, making the forest floor dark, and finding your way through dense undergrowth can be a slow, exhausting job. Deep rivers that are difficult and dangerous to cross, biting insects and diseases such as malaria are additional hazards. But the jungle habitat is incredibly diverse, with thousands of different species living close together, which makes this one of the most rewarding environments to explore.

Forest in Brunei

Scientists on the 1991 to 1992 Brunei Rainforest Project look at the forest from their boats. A team of 90 scientists studied a large area of forest, much of it undisturbed by humans, and took part in a variety of botanical, zoological and geographical projects.

Habitat under threat

The world's rainforests are shrinking, largely because local people rely on the timber industry for their income. Explorers play a vital role in studying, recording and protecting these important habitats. Thanks to their work, we now know far more about the jungle, and many useful discoveries are coming to light – from new animal species to types of plants that can be used in medicines.

Antarctic camp

These polar explorers have made a camp in the snow. They are setting up a Global Positioning System (GPS), which links to satellites orbiting the earth, to give an accurate reading of their position. There are no signs and few landmarks in the polar regions to guide explorers.

Polar exploration

In the polar regions, the Arctic and Antarctic, explorers have to cope with some of the most difficult conditions of all. Temperatures regularly go below –50°C and howling winds create severe blizzards. So anyone travelling in the polar regions needs to wear the right clothes. Polar explorers wear several layers of clothes, covering the entire body, that allow good ventilation but at the same time keep in warmth. It is also vital to travel light to move around more easily in these harsh conditions. Glaciers, snowdrifts and deep crevasses make travelling especially difficult – even with skis, skidoos or sledges, progress is usually slow. Above all, the explorer must learn to respect this difficult terrain.

Desert exploration

There are several different types of desert – some sandy, some rocky, others supporting scrubby vegetation – but they all have very low rainfall. Since there is no cloud cover, the temperature is baking hot during the day and very cold at night. There can be virtually no water, shade or shelter, and sandstorms are a problem in many deserts. Desert travellers wear strong, lightweight clothes that protect them from the sun and wind. Desert equipment also has to stand up to these harsh conditions. A good supply of drinking water is vital. Equally, desert explorers try to lose as little body fluid as possible, so they work in the evening when it is cooler and they are less likely to sweat.

In the sand

These scientists are analyzing desert soils and researching the plants that grow in them to find out more about desert habitats that cover more than a third of the earth's land surface. Reports on global warming suggest that temperatures are rising around the world and more land will become desert.

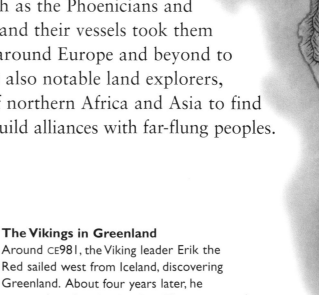

Greenland

Brattahlid

NORTH
AMERICA

Newfoundland

ATLANTIC OCEAN

SOUTH
AMERICA

Empire and trade
For the Romans and other early peoples, there was often more than one reason to explore. While sending out cargo ships such as this one to expand their trade networks, they were also looking for lands to conquer.

EARLY EXPLORERS

People have always been explorers, fascinated by what is over the next hill or around the next headland. Our ancient Stone Age ancestors were constantly on the move, looking for new sources of food and new land to farm. By the time of the first great European civilizations, such as the ancient Greeks of the 5th century BCE, people were travelling further, finding places where they could start new colonies or find valuable goods to trade. Coastal peoples such as the Phoenicians and Vikings became great shipbuilders, and their vessels took them on long, often dangerous, voyages around Europe and beyond to Africa and America. But there were also notable land explorers, travellers who braved the deserts of northern Africa and Asia to find new routes, carry trade goods and build alliances with far-flung peoples.

The Vikings in Greenland
Around CE981, the Viking leader Erik the Red sailed west from Iceland, discovering Greenland. About four years later, he returned to the island to live. The remains of one of his settlements, Brattahlid, can still be seen in southern Greenland. His son, Leif Eriksson, sailed to Newfoundland from here.

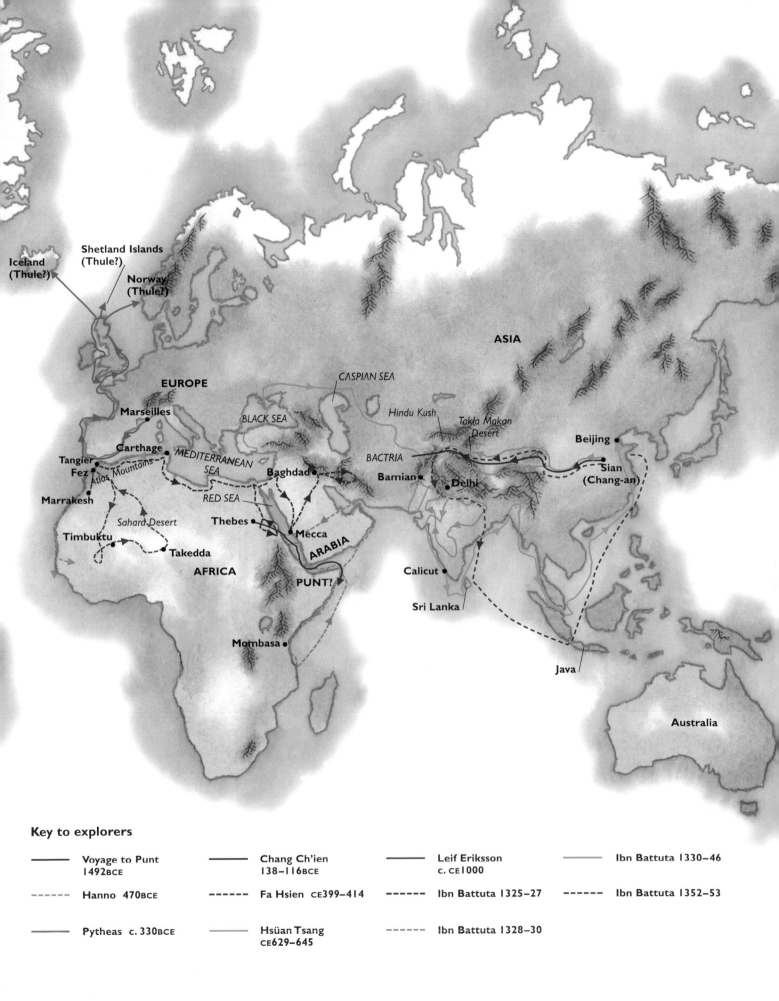

Iceland (Thule?)

Shetland Islands (Thule?)

Norway (Thule?)

ASIA

EUROPE

CASPIAN SEA

Marseilles

BLACK SEA

Hindu Kush

Takla Makan Desert

Beijing

Carthage

MEDITERRANEAN SEA

BACTRIA

Tangier

Atlas Mountains

Baghdad

Bamian

Delhi

Sian (Chang-an)

Fez

RED SEA

Marrakesh

Sahara Desert

Thebes

Timbuktu

Takedda

Mecca

ARABIA

Calicut

AFRICA

PUNT?

Sri Lanka

Mombasa

Java

Australia

Key to explorers

——	Voyage to Punt 1492BCE	——	Chang Ch'ien 138–116BCE	——	Leif Eriksson c. CE1000	——	Ibn Battuta 1330–46
- - - -	Hanno 470BCE	- - - -	Fa Hsien CE399–414	- - - -	Ibn Battuta 1325–27	- - - -	Ibn Battuta 1352–53
——	Pytheas c. 330BCE	——	Hsüan Tsang CE629–645	- - - -	Ibn Battuta 1328–30		

Mediterranean traders and explorers

Greek explorers

The Greeks explored the coasts of the Aegean Sea, where they set up colonies. In around 330BCE, the explorer Pytheas sailed out from Marseilles into the north Atlantic Ocean as far as a place he called Thule – perhaps Norway, Iceland or the Shetland Islands.

The lands around the Mediterranean Sea were home to some of the greatest early civilizations, such as the Egyptians, Greeks, Phoenicians and Romans. Many of these peoples settled by the sea and could travel more easily along the coasts than across the rocky, often mountainous, country inland. They traded with people on the Mediterranean coasts and islands, and then sailed further in search of new customers, out into the cold, inhospitable waters of the Atlantic Ocean.

Phoenician travellers

The Phoenicians traded all around the Aegean, the Mediterranean and the Black Sea. Their most famous explorer was Hanno, who came from a colony in North Africa called Carthage. In 470BCE, Hanno sailed far down the coast of West Africa where he found 'a country smelling of spices from which fiery rivers fall into the sea, and the land is so hot that men are not able to go in it'.

Phoenician ship

Murex shell

Trade goods

One of the most valuable Phoenician cargoes was the rare Tyrian purple dye made from a snail called the murex. Only rich people could afford the dye because hundreds of snails were needed to make even a small amount.

Ships of the Mediterranean
The Mediterranean explorers used wooden ships that usually had both oars and square sails, so they could deal with all sorts of conditions – shallow and deep waters, windy and calm weather. Ships were steered by a large oar in the stern.

On the march
In the 4th century BCE, the Macedonians, under Alexander the Great, travelled over 32,000km and carved out an empire that extended from Egypt to the borders of India. By the 2nd century CE, the Romans (shown above in Romania) had marched right across Europe, conquering most of the land between North Africa and Britain. They also made detailed surveys and built roads, thus giving greater access to huge areas of land.

Voyage to Punt
In 1492BCE, the Egyptian queen Hatshepsut sent a fleet of ships on a voyage from the Red Sea to a country called Punt, which was probably in East Africa. When they returned from Punt, they brought back ivory, ebony, gold, spices and creatures such as baboons.

13

The Great Buddha of Bamian
On his route to India from China, the Buddhist traveller Hsüan Tsang reached Bamian, a religious centre in what is now Afghanistan. Here, he was amazed by the colossal gilded statue of the Buddha, 53m high, cut into the cliff. He said that the statue was 'glittering with gold that dazzled the eyes'. The Bamian Buddha was destroyed by the Taliban in 2001.

The empire of China

From the 2nd century BCE onwards, China had a huge empire that stretched from the Yellow Sea far westwards to the Yangtze River and beyond. Most of the big cities, such as Chang-an and Nanking, were in the east, and many travellers set out west from these centres. Some went to trade, some on diplomatic missions for the emperor, others on religious quests.

Chang Ch'ien

The earliest-known Chinese explorer was Chang Ch'ien, who worked for the emperor, Wu Ti. In 138BCE, Wu Ti sent Chang on a long journey west to search for allies who would help him fight the nomadic peoples, such as the Huns, who were attacking the empire. Chang journeyed west, but was captured by the Huns and imprisoned for ten years. Eventually, he escaped and travelled to Bactria (northern Afghanistan). He did not find any allies, but he discovered a useful trade route that would eventually become known as the Silk Road.

The Hindu Kush
The Hindu Kush is a mountainous area in north-west Afghanistan. Travellers heading west or south from Central Asia had to pass through the region, which was home to several nomadic peoples. Explorers and locals alike travelled through high mountain passes between desolate rocky slopes.

Buddhist explorers

Some of the greatest explorers were Buddhist monks and scholars, who travelled in search of relics, sacred sites and religious books. Fa Hsien journeyed across Central Asia and through north-east India before sailing to Sri Lanka in CE399–414. In the mid 7th century, another Chinese Buddhist, Hsüan Tsang, travelled all around India, bringing home some 700 religious books and many statues of the Buddha.

The Takla Makan Desert
Both Fa Hsien and Hsüan Tsang had to cross this desert. It was a lonely place, and even today its stony ground supports little life apart from camels. Fa Hsien followed a trail of human bones across the empty landscape, hoping that he would survive the crossing of this barren country.

Heavenly horse
In Ferghana (Uzbekistan), Chang Ch'ien admired the local horses, which the Chinese later imported. The emperor called them 'celestial' (heavenly) horses, and Han sculptors made fine statues of them.

The Vikings

From their homelands in
northern Europe, the Vikings
explored far and wide. From
the 8th century CE, there was
a shortage of good farmland in Scandinavia and people
found it hard to make a living, so many Vikings took to
their ships and explored. Some went raiding, stealing what
they could from the people of Europe's coastal villages.
Other Vikings were peaceful explorers. They traded in
furs, whalebone and walrus ivory, and established new
villages where they found land to farm.

Leif Eriksson
In about CE1000, Leif Eriksson
discovered a land he called Vinland,
which was probably Newfoundland.
He was among the first Europeans
to reach the Americas.

Compass
By lining up the needle
with the sun at noon,
Viking sailors could
find where north lay.
They could then work
out the direction in
which they were sailing.

Iceland
The first Viking to settle in Iceland was Ingolf Arnesson, who arrived in around 870 in search of land to farm. Thousands of Vikings followed him in the late 9th and 10th centuries. They built sturdy wooden houses, which had no windows and turf roofs to keep them warm.

Seamen and settlers
The Vikings sailed along the coasts of western Europe and travelled far up rivers such as the Danube. But their most daring voyages were into the stormy, unknown waters of the north Atlantic. By around 1000, there were Vikings living in Britain, Ireland, Normandy, Italy and Russia. In their search for new lands to settle, they found Iceland, Greenland and even North America. The American coast was so bleak that one Viking thought the whole coast 'seemed to be covered with a single slab of rock'.

Land ahoy!
A typical Viking ship had a large square sail, which gave it plenty of speed in good wind on an open sea. The sailors used oars when the wind dropped or for rowing in shallow waters. These Vikings are also carrying their animals to settle in the new land.

Great axe
The axe was a favourite Viking weapon, but this one is so beautifully decorated that it was probably not used in war. A Viking chief would have carried it to show his great power.

Travelling with a caravan
By the 14th century, when Ibn Battuta was alive, caravans of camels regularly crossed the Sahara, carrying salt and manufactured goods to important trading centres such as Timbuktu. Ibn Battuta joined such a caravan when he journeyed east from Timbuktu.

Muslim travellers

The Islamic faith was first revealed to the prophet Mohammed in the Arabian peninsula in the 7th century CE. Soon, the followers of Islam, who are known as Muslims, were travelling far and wide, spreading their faith. Many Muslims were also merchants, so they had two powerful reasons for travelling – for religion and for trade. The greatest of all the early Muslim travellers was the explorer Ibn Battuta who made land journeys through Arabia, Western Asia and India, and sailed to China. But he is most famous for his travels across Africa's Sahara Desert. Towards the end of his life he wrote a book, *The Travels of Ibn Battuta*, describing his adventures.

On the water
Ibn Battuta used several different types of boat, including a dug-out canoe made from a tree trunk. At sea, he travelled in a dhow, a slender vessel with triangular sails, which was capable of travelling great distances.

Crossing the Sahara

Ibn Battuta travelled south from his home in Tangier, passing through the city of Fez and journeying across the vast Sahara. He coped with sandstorms, snowstorms and the Atlas Mountains on the way. Eventually, he reached and explored the Niger River, before arriving at the great trading city of Timbuktu. From here he headed east to another trading town, Takedda, before going north, towards Fez. Along the way, Ibn Battuta saw many wonders, such as a village of houses built from blocks of salt, and observed many of the customs of the local people he met.

Muslim learning
Many Muslim scholars were experts in astronomy and navigation. This scholar is showing his pupils an astrolabe, an instrument used to measure the height of a star, to help work out latitude (distance from the equator). Muslim craft workers made the world's most accurate astrolabes.

Hippos on the Niger
Ibn Battuta was fascinated when he saw hippos, but he could not have seen them too clearly because he wrote that they 'have manes and tails, and their heads are like horses' heads'.

THE SEARCH FOR TRADE ROUTES

From the Middle Ages, more and more explorers tried to open up new trade routes. In Europe, there was a huge demand for spices from Indonesia and materials such as silk from China. A few European travellers reached China by land, but many more tried to find the fastest sea-route from Europe to the East. Some sailed around Africa, exploring the coast as they went. A few looked for shorter, but more perilous, routes through the icy waters of the Arctic. Other explorers, such as the navigator Christopher Columbus, sailed westwards across the Atlantic Ocean trying to reach China, but discovered America instead.

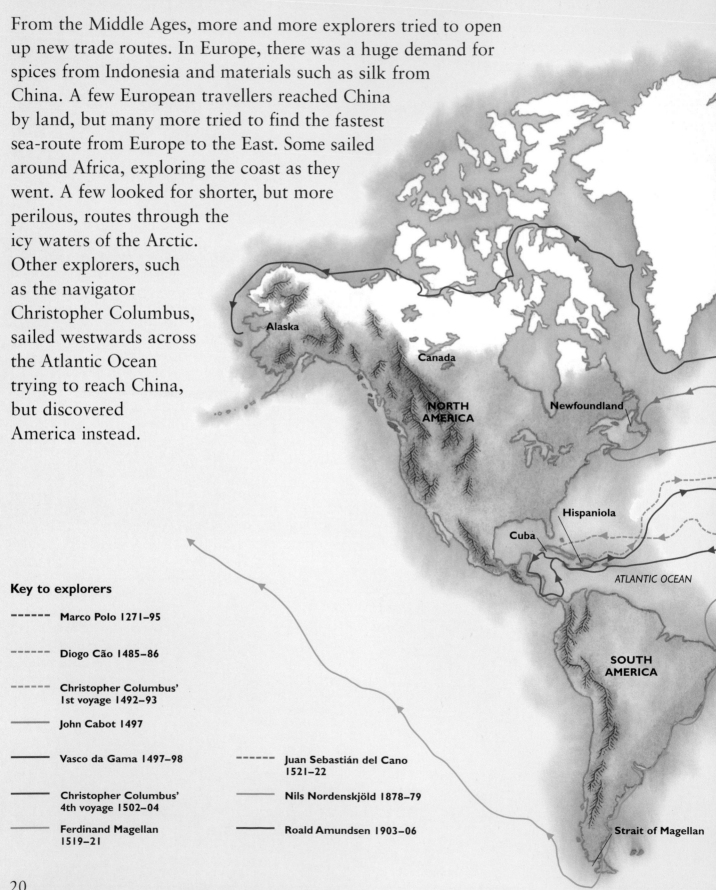

Alaska

Canada

NORTH
AMERICA

Newfoundland

Hispaniola

Cuba

ATLANTIC OCEAN

SOUTH
AMERICA

Strait of Magellan

Key to explorers

- - - - - - **Marco Polo 1271–95**

- - - - - - **Diogo Cão 1485–86**

- - - - - - **Christopher Columbus'
1st voyage 1492–93**

――― **John Cabot 1497**

――― **Vasco da Gama 1497–98**

――― **Christopher Columbus'
4th voyage 1502–04**

――― **Ferdinand Magellan
1519–21**

- - - - - - **Juan Sebastián del Cano
1521–22**

――― **Nils Nordenskjöld 1878–79**

――― **Roald Amundsen 1903–06**

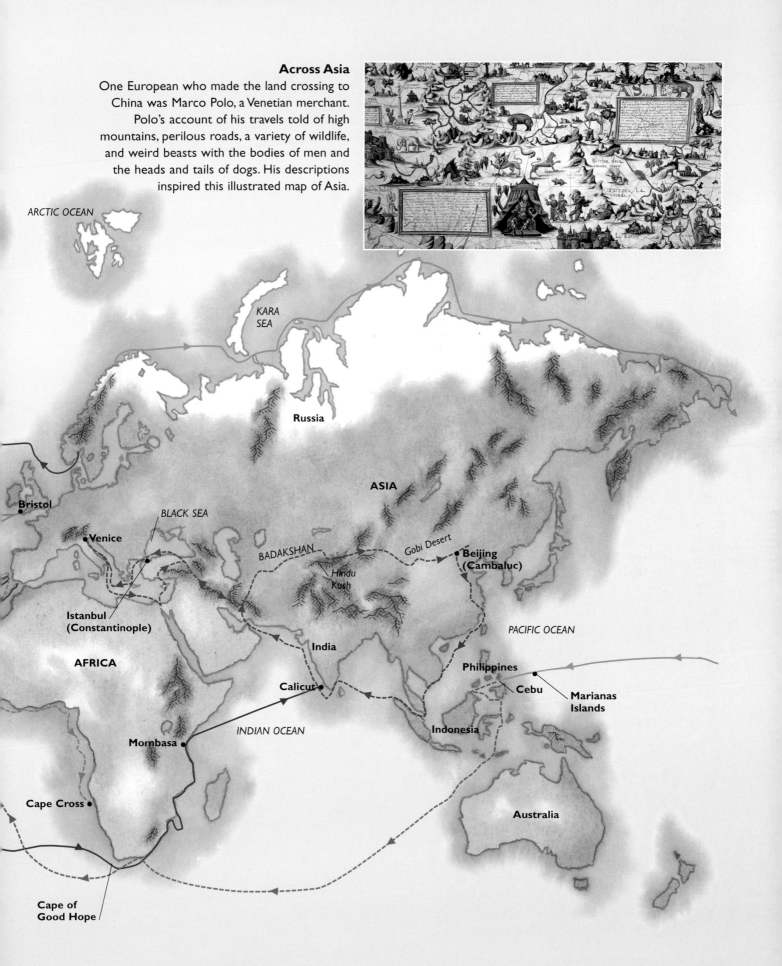

Across Asia

One European who made the land crossing to China was Marco Polo, a Venetian merchant. Polo's account of his travels told of high mountains, perilous roads, a variety of wildlife, and weird beasts with the bodies of men and the heads and tails of dogs. His descriptions inspired this illustrated map of Asia.

ARCTIC OCEAN

KARA SEA

Russia

Bristol

BLACK SEA

Venice

ASIA

BADAKSHAN

Gobi Desert

Beijing (Cambaluc)

Hindu Kush

Istanbul (Constantinople)

PACIFIC OCEAN

India

AFRICA

Calicut

Philippines

Cebu

Marianas Islands

INDIAN OCEAN

Indonesia

Mombasa

Cape Cross

Australia

Cape of Good Hope

The Silk Road

In ancient times, the only people who knew how to make silk were the Chinese. Many people in Europe wanted to buy this luxurious cloth, and merchants from China carried silk all the way across Asia to sell in cities such as Constantinople (Istanbul) or Trebizond (Trabzon) on the Black Sea. The long route from China, across the Gobi Desert and through the mountains of the Hindu Kush, was called the Silk Road. Few Europeans were able to travel to China along the Silk Road until the 13th century, when the Mongols conquered Central Asia. Soon after, merchants and missionaries braved the long and perilous journey.

The secret of silk
Silk workers spin into thread the material unravelled from silk moth cocoons. For centuries, the Chinese told no one how they made silk. They could then charge high prices, knowing that European merchants could not get silk elsewhere.

At the court of Kublai Khan
Venetian merchants Niccolo Polo, his brother Maffeo and son Marco visited Emperor Kublai Khan at Cambaluc (Beijing). Marco described the palace interior as 'all ablaze with scarlet and green and blue and yellow'. Niccolo introduced Marco as 'your servant' and Kublai took him at his word. Marco worked for the emperor for 20 years.

The road to China
The Polos left their home city, Venice, in 1271. Most of their journey to China was by land. They rode on horseback, but their baggage was carried by camels and donkeys. The difficult 8,000km journey took more than three years because Marco fell ill – the Polos stayed in Badakshan, Afghanistan, for a year until he recovered.

The Franciscan friars
Among the first Europeans to travel along the Silk Road were Franciscan friars, who went to Asia in the mid 13th century. One friar, William Rubruck, travelled in a covered wagon all the way to Karakorum, the court of the Mongol emperor. By the time he returned, he had covered some 17,700km.

A rocky road
The Silk Road was actually a collection of narrow, boulder-strewn tracks stretching across Central Asia, from Beijing in China to the Black Sea. It was a hard route, crossing deserts and mountains, but China's merchants were prepared to take the risk, so it was busy with traders bringing rich cargoes to the West. They made handsome profits, as did the merchants who bought their goods. But few Europeans knew much about the Silk Road until the Polos returned. After they got back, Marco was imprisoned by enemies from Genoa. He told a fellow prisoner, called Rustichello, all about his journeys, and Rustichello published a book, *The Travels of Marco Polo*. Some of Rustichello's stories were far-fetched, but they gave European traders the knowledge to access the Silk Road and discover the riches of the East.

Around the Cape of Good Hope

For much of the Middle Ages Portugal was ruled by the Moors, Muslim people from North Africa. But in the 15th century, the Portuguese reconquered their country and chased the Moors back to their African homeland. Portuguese sailors heard tales of great gold mines deep within Africa, and they began to navigate the African coast in search of riches. To begin with, seamen such as Diogo Cão explored the shores and inlets of West Africa. They soon reached Africa's southernmost point, the Cape of Good Hope, and were on their way east towards India.

The Cape of Good Hope
The rocky tip of South Africa was beaten by storms when Bartolomeu Dias and his crew rounded it in 1488. Dias was the first to show that a route to India around the tip of Africa was possible.

The Portuguese navigators

Portugal became a great sea power during the time of Prince Henry the Navigator (1394–1460), a notable naval commander who paid for many expeditions. Henry's shipbuilders developed the caravel – a small, light sailing ship that was ideal for exploration. Caravels could carry lateen (triangular) sails for coastal waters, or be square-rigged for sailing on the open sea. Portuguese navigators, such as Cão and Dias, sailed caravels. But the most successful Portuguese sailor was trader and explorer Vasco da Gama. In 1497, da Gama rounded the Cape of Good Hope and battled with storms and currents to sail up the coast of East Africa to Mombasa. He then crossed the Indian Ocean, becoming the first European to reach India by sea. Da Gama did not profit from trade with India, but he blazed a trail that was soon followed by other Portuguese traders.

Henry the Navigator
Prince Henry founded a school of navigation and built an observatory. His sailors rediscovered the Azores, the Madeira Islands and the Cape Verde Islands.

Charting the oceans
Early mariners used maps called portolan charts. These were drawn on a grid of criss-crossing lines radiating from compass points. The lines indicated compass bearings and helped show a sailor which bearing he needed to follow. These huge charts were drawn on parchment made of goat- or sheepskin.

Along the coast
Diogo Cão looks at the African coast from the bow of his caravel. In 1485, he sailed all the way to Cape Cross on the coast of Namibia, much further south than any previous European sailor and far beyond the edge of his chart.

The West Indies

Amerigo Vespucci
A businessman from Florence, Vespucci explored the eastern coast of South America in 1499–1500 and 1501–1502.

In the late 15th century, European merchants grew rich trading in spices from the islands they called the East Indies or Spice Islands (Indonesia). But the sea journey around Africa to the Indies was lengthy and dangerous, and they longed to find a quicker, easier route. Explorers such as Christopher Columbus, a sailor from Genoa, Italy, insisted that, since the world was round, it should be possible to reach the Indies by sailing across the Atlantic Ocean. But no one knew that the Americas stood in the way. When Columbus sailed west in 1492, he discovered not the Indies, but the islands of Cuba, San Salvador and Hispaniola – what we now call the West Indies.

The American continent

Christopher Columbus and John Cabot, the explorers who crossed the Atlantic at this time, were convinced that they had discovered a group of islands off the eastern coast of China. But one explorer, Amerigo Vespucci, had a different view. Sailing far along the coast of Brazil, Vespucci realized that he had found not one of a group of islands, but a landmass large enough to be a continent. Some experts believe that the name of the continent, America, is based on Vespucci's first name.

Claiming the Pacific
Vasco Núñez de Balboa, a Spaniard, crossed Panama in 1513 and was the first European to see the Pacific from America. He claimed the ocean for Spain.

Natural riches
Columbus wrote that the New World had 'fine green trees, streams everywhere, and different kinds of fruit'. Local plants such as pineapples and potatoes were unknown in Europe.

John Cabot
Sailing from the British port of Bristol in 1497, spice trader and navigator John Cabot crossed the north Atlantic and explored the coast of Newfoundland. The cod he brought back attracted fishermen to this coast.

The voyages of Columbus

Although Columbus was born in Italy, his expeditions were paid for by the king and queen of Spain, Ferdinand and Isabella, so Columbus claimed the islands he discovered for Spain. Columbus sailed four times to the West Indies. On the first journey, he discovered Watling Island, Cuba and Hispaniola. His second trip took him to Jamaica. On the third voyage, he sailed via Trinidad to Hispaniola. He explored the Central American coast on his final trip.

The *Santa Maria*

Columbus' flagship on his first voyage, the *Santa Maria*, was only around 30m long (scarcely large enough for a crew of about 40 men) but the vessel's square sails and stout timbers took them all the way across the Atlantic.

Circling the globe

In September 1522, a small ship, the *Victoria*, arrived in the harbour at Seville, Spain. The vessel and its tiny crew of 18 men were all that was left of a large, five-ship expedition begun by navigator Ferdinand Magellan in 1519. It was the first ship to sail all the way around the world. The reason for Magellan's journey was trade. In 1494, a treaty had divided the Atlantic Ocean and lands on either side of it – Portugal was given the rights to trade in the east, Spain the west. However, who had the right to trade with the Spice Islands, halfway around the world, was in dispute. Magellan, sailing for Spain, set off west hoping he could reach the Spice Islands via the Americas, and so began the most amazing sea journey of his time.

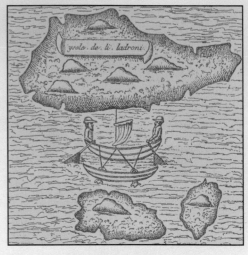

Pigafetta's book
We know about Magellan's expedition because of an Italian who sailed with him, Antonio Pigafetta. Pigafetta was one of the men who made it back to Europe. He wrote a book about the journey, *The First Voyage Around the Globe*, which was illustrated with maps and pictures of the ships.

The death of Magellan
After taking 100 days to cross the Pacific, Magellan arrived in the Marianas Islands, where he fought with the inhabitants after they stole one of his boats. They sailed on to Cebu, in the Philippines, where the people seemed more peaceful. The king of Cebu converted to Christianity and agreed to accept the rule of Spain. But many of the local people were unhappy about this and fought the Europeans. Magellan was wounded and died on the shore as his men ran back to their ships.

Magellan's expedition

After crossing the Atlantic, Magellan survived a mutiny, but one of his five ships was wrecked off Patagonia. Then, while searching for a route into the Pacific, one of his ships deserted and returned to Spain, but Magellan found the strait leading into the ocean. The Pacific was larger than Magellan had thought, and they ran out of food. Pigafetta wrote that they ate rats, leather and 'old biscuits, all full of worms'. Many men died of starvation and others were in a poor way when they reached the Philippines, where Magellan was killed. The remaining crew took two ships and sailed west to reach the Spice Islands in 1521. Only one of these, the *Victoria* and its navigator, Juan Sebastián del Cano, finally braved the storms of the Indian Ocean to return to Spain in 1522.

Sir Francis Drake
English navigator Sir Francis Drake completed a second voyage around the world in 1580. Drake, a skilled seaman, spent much of his life raiding the ships of England's enemy, Spain, and made a huge profit for his sponsors.

29

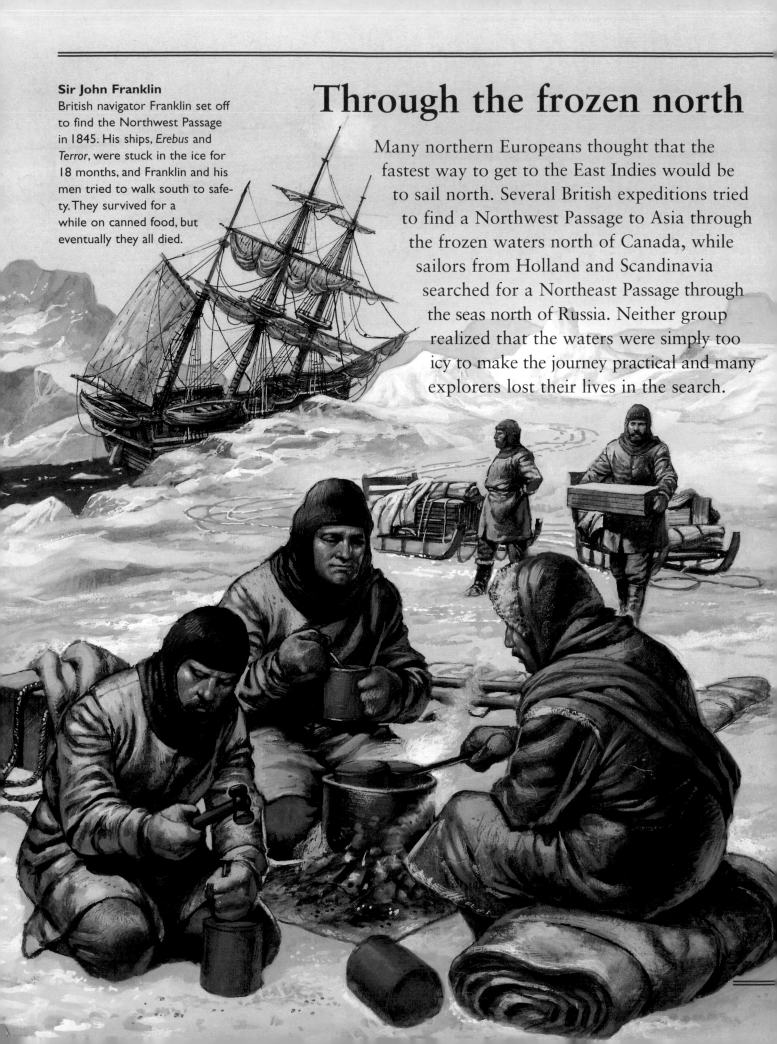

Sir John Franklin
British navigator Franklin set off to find the Northwest Passage in 1845. His ships, *Erebus* and *Terror*, were stuck in the ice for 18 months, and Franklin and his men tried to walk south to safety. They survived for a while on canned food, but eventually they all died.

Through the frozen north

Many northern Europeans thought that the fastest way to get to the East Indies would be to sail north. Several British expeditions tried to find a Northwest Passage to Asia through the frozen waters north of Canada, while sailors from Holland and Scandinavia searched for a Northeast Passage through the seas north of Russia. Neither group realized that the waters were simply too icy to make the journey practical and many explorers lost their lives in the search.

Nordenskjöld

Finnish scientist and explorer Nils Nordenskjöld made it through the Northeast Passage between 1878 and 1879. He knew he was likely to succeed when he rounded Cape Chelyuskin, the northernmost point in Asia and a major staging post on the way. He and his crew put up a monument at the Cape to celebrate their achievement.

Franklin's goggles

From snow-goggles to sleds, Sir John Franklin was well-equipped on his ill-fated trip into the Northwest Passage. These snow-goggles are made of leather and were worn to protect the eyes from the glare of bright sun reflecting off the snow.

Finding Passages to the East

The search for the Northwest Passage began during the 15th and 16th centuries, with explorers such as the Bristol navigator John Cabot (see p26) and the adventurer Martin Frobisher. Along with later navigators such as Sir John Franklin, these men found out much about the seas and lands north of Canada. But it was not until 1903 to 1906, with the expedition of Norwegian explorer Roald Amundsen in his ship the *Gjöa* that anyone made it through the Northwest Passage. The Northeast Passage also had its pioneers, including the Russian Semyon Dezhnev. Again success came to a Scandinavian, Nils Nordenskjöld, whose triumph was due to a lot of experience of Arctic waters and a ship, the *Vega*, which had a specially reinforced hull.

Willem Barents

Dutch navigator Willem Barents made several attempts to find the Northeast Passage in the late 16th century. On his last voyage, in 1596, he rediscovered the island of Spitsbergen before reaching the Kara Sea, where his ship became trapped in the ice. Barents and his crew built a wooden hut for winter quarters. The following year, they tried to sail back to the Russian mainland in small boats, but Barents died on the way.

To the North Pole by balloon
In 1897, Swedish balloonist Salomon-Auguste Andreé took off from Spitsbergen for the North Pole. His huge hydrogen balloon drifted out of control for almost three days before coming down. Andreé and his two companions were forced to leave the balloon's enclosed gondola and continue the journey on foot, dragging their equipment on a sledge. Three months later, they reached Franz Josef Land, but died before they could be rescued. Their bodies — and Andreé's expedition diary — were found by a scientific expedition 33 years later.

NEW HORIZONS

From the 16th century onwards, European countries began to build up huge empires in different parts of the world – Spain, France and Britain had colonies in the Americas, and the Dutch ruled large parts of South-east Asia. Several countries – Britain, France, Italy, Germany, Portugal, Spain and Belgium – took over areas of Africa. Explorers travelled to all these places, trading, settling, trying to convert the local people to Christianity or simply blazing a trail for those who came after them. In the process, Europeans learned about some of the world's most spectacular places – from the lakes and forests of Canada to the high Andes Mountains in South America. Soon the search for new horizons took them still further, and they got to know the unique scenery and wildlife of Australia, and the inhospitable icy territories at the poles.

Across Antarctica
In 2001, Ann Bancroft from the USA and Liv Arnesen from Norway became the first women to cross Antarctica on skis. The two women pulled packs weighing about 250kg each on their 2,763km journey. The trek through sub-zero temperatures and howling gales took 94 days. Most of the time Bancroft and Arnesen travelled on their cross-country skis, but when the wind was in the right direction, specially designed parasails pulled them along.

The search for El Dorado

Many Spanish sailors visited Central America after Christopher Columbus' first voyage in 1492. They soon discovered that Mexico was home to an advanced civilization, the Aztecs, who built big cities, and made stunning jewellery out of gold and other precious metals. They also heard rumours of yet more riches in South America, and of a country so wealthy that their king's entire skin was covered in gold dust. This mythical figure was 'El Dorado', and explorers soon set out to find his kingdom.

Exploring South America

——— Cortés 1519–21

------ Pizarro 1532

——— Almagro 1535–37

——— Orellana 1540

——— Valdivia 1541–47

Tenochtitlán

Quito

Cajamarca

Cuzco

Amazon

Atacama Desert

Andes Mountains

Valdivia

Spanish explorers
Several of Pizarro's captains were notable explorers. Francisco de Orellana followed the Amazon River, Diego de Almagro crossed the Atacama Desert, and Pedro de Valdivia marched south into Chile.

A king's ransom
Pizarro captured the Inca ruler, Atahualpa, and the Inca people brought thousands of gold objects for Atahualpa's ransom. However, Pizarro did not release the ruler, but had him killed after falsely accusing him of treachery.

Out with the idols
Both Cortés and Pizarro hoped to convert the people they conquered to Christianity, and Roman Catholic priests followed in the conquerors' footsteps. Cortés used this as an excuse to destroy many of the statues of the Aztec gods that decorated the temples of Mexico.

The conquistadores

Although they did not find El Dorado, Spanish conquerors, or conquistadores, quickly plundered the empires of the Aztecs in Mexico and the Incas of Peru. In Mexico, the Spanish forces were led by nobleman Hernan Cortés, who completed his conquest between 1519 and 1521 with help from some Mexican enemies of the Aztecs. Francisco Pizarro, with only 200 soldiers, conquered Peru in 1531 to 1533. In the major battle of Cajamarca, a peaceful meeting turned into a massacre when Pizarro's men attacked a horde of unarmed Incas.

The Aztec capital

Cortés was amazed by the splendour of Mexico's capital, Tenochtitlán. The capital, on the site of modern Mexico City, was in the middle of a huge lake. Cortés described a central square so large that 'a town of five hundred people could easily be built within its walls'.

Europeans in North America

Europeans who travelled to North America from the 16th century onwards were amazed by the range of landscapes, from great lakes and fast-flowing rivers to high mountains and dense forests. To find their way, European explorers learned about the country from local people. Many travellers were fur trappers, who followed local tracks and trails. Other pioneers, such as French explorer Robert Cavelier de La Salle, kept to the lakes and rivers, using native-style canoes to find good trade routes. By the 17th century, both Britain and France had established colonies in Canada.

Across the lakes
French explorer Samuel de Champlain helped establish the French colony in Canada. With the help of native American guides, he explored the Atlantic coast and found a route inland by sailing up rivers to the Great Lakes.

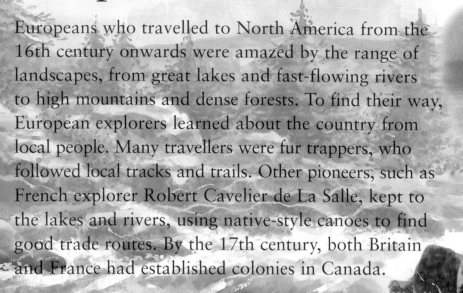

Lewis and Clark
In 1803, the USA bought the vast territory of Louisiana from France. Thomas Jefferson, the US president, sent Meriwether Lewis and William Clark to explore the territory and find a route to the Pacific Ocean. Between 1804 and 1806, the pair canoed along the Missouri, Yellowstone and Columbia rivers.

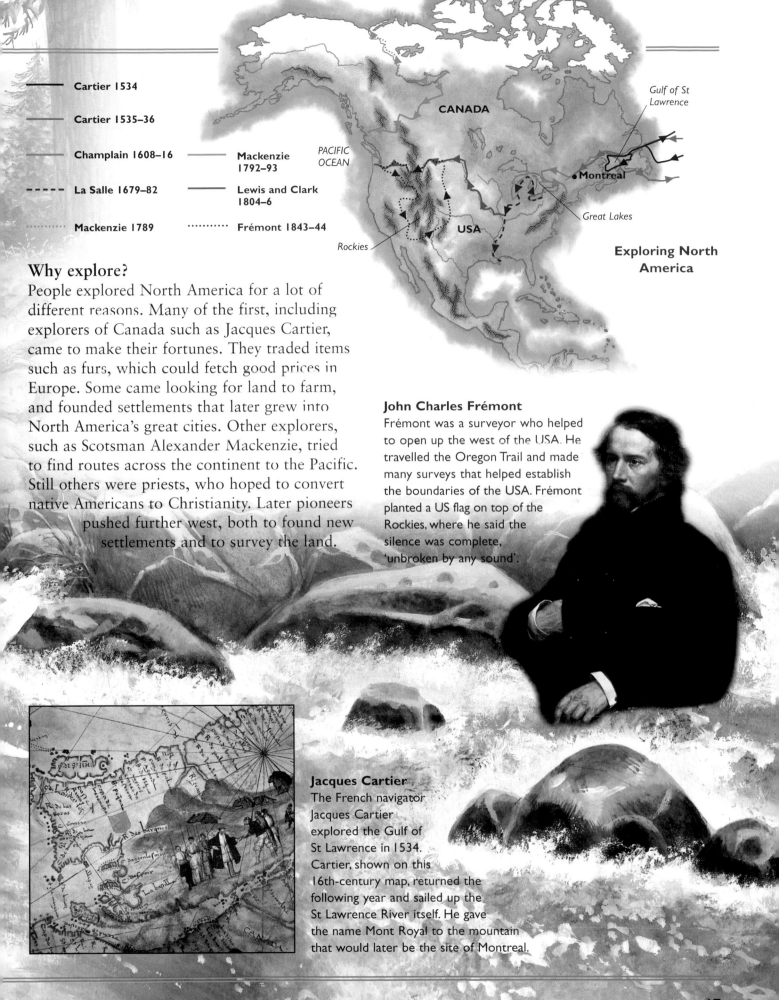

Cartier 1534

Cartier 1535–36

Champlain 1608–16

La Salle 1679–82

Mackenzie 1789

Mackenzie 1792–93

Lewis and Clark 1804–6

Frémont 1843–44

Exploring North America

CANADA

PACIFIC OCEAN

USA

Montreal

Gulf of St Lawrence

Great Lakes

Rockies

Why explore?

People explored North America for a lot of different reasons. Many of the first, including explorers of Canada such as Jacques Cartier, came to make their fortunes. They traded items such as furs, which could fetch good prices in Europe. Some came looking for land to farm, and founded settlements that later grew into North America's great cities. Other explorers, such as Scotsman Alexander Mackenzie, tried to find routes across the continent to the Pacific. Still others were priests, who hoped to convert native Americans to Christianity. Later pioneers pushed further west, both to found new settlements and to survey the land.

John Charles Frémont
Frémont was a surveyor who helped to open up the west of the USA. He travelled the Oregon Trail and made many surveys that helped establish the boundaries of the USA. Frémont planted a US flag on top of the Rockies, where he said the silence was complete, 'unbroken by any sound'.

Jacques Cartier
The French navigator Jacques Cartier explored the Gulf of St Lawrence in 1534. Cartier, shown on this 16th-century map, returned the following year and sailed up the St Lawrence River itself. He gave the name Mont Royal to the mountain that would later be the site of Montreal.

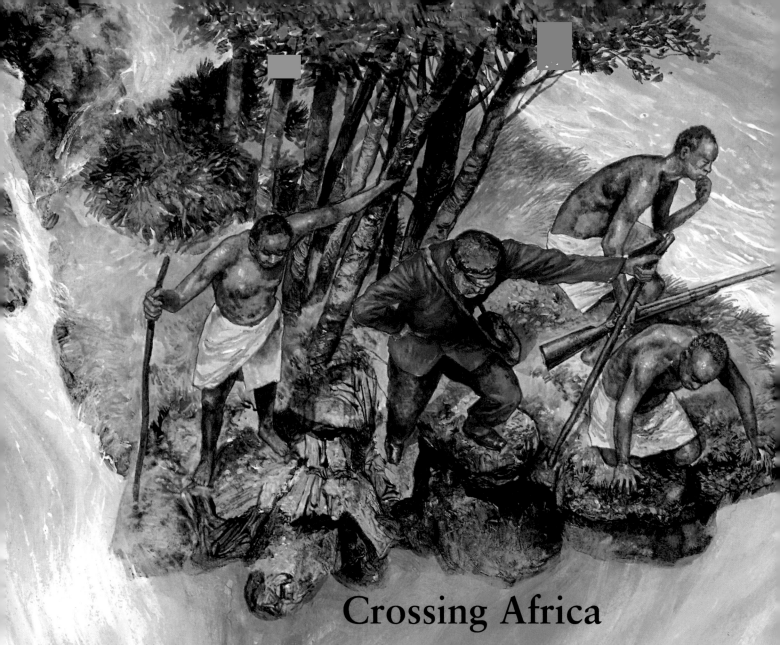

Crossing Africa

For Europeans and Americans in the 18th century, Africa was a vast and mysterious continent. They knew it only as a source of slave labour, and had little idea about what the interior of Africa was like. The 19th-century explorers such as the German Heinrich Barth, who crossed the Sahara Desert, and Britons Richard Burton and John Hanning Speke, who explored the Nile River, began to open European eyes to Africa. Best-known of the explorers of Africa was Scottish missionary David Livingstone. He crossed southern Africa, following the courses of rivers and discovering several great lakes. He also alerted Europeans to the evils of slavery.

Timbuktu
In 1828, Frenchman René Caillié became the first European to return alive from Timbuktu and describe the fabled city. To get there, he crossed the Sahara Desert from the coast of Guinea with a caravan of camels and journeyed in disguise, wearing Arab dress.

Speke's notebook
John Hanning Speke drew beautiful illustrations of the wildlife he saw on his journeys through East Africa.

At Victoria Falls
Explorer David Livingstone saw how the 1,600m-wide Zambezi River plunged into a gap that was only about 20m across. The result was rushing, churning water and great clouds of spray.

Victoria Falls

Livingstone travelled widely in southern Africa before making his famous journey across the continent in 1853 to 1856. Following the Zambezi River, Livingstone found the Victoria Falls, and named them after Britain's queen. Leaving his canoe, he stood on an island in the river, watching the water plunging over 100m down. He said later: 'Scenes so lovely must have been gazed upon by angels in their flight'.

Richard Burton
Burton explored the Arabian peninsula before setting off with Speke to search for the source of the Nile River in East Africa. The pair discovered Lake Tanganyika in 1858.

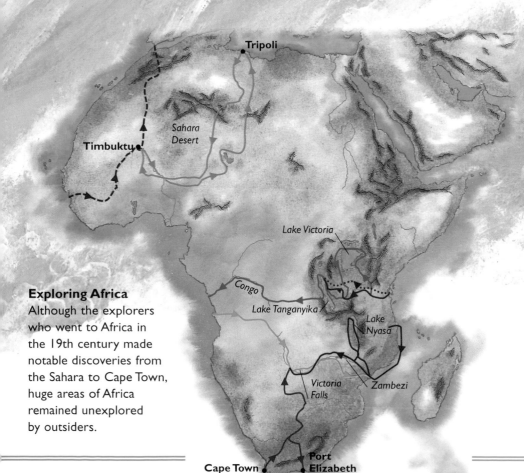

Exploring Africa

Although the explorers who went to Africa in the 19th century made notable discoveries from the Sahara to Cape Town, huge areas of Africa remained unexplored by outsiders.

Exploring Africa

- – – – – – – Caillié 1827–28
- ———————— Barth 1850–55
- ———————— Burton and Speke 1857–58
- ················ Stanley 1871–72
- ———————— Stanley 1874–77
- ———————— Livingstone 1849–51
- ———————— Livingstone 1853–56
- ———————— Livingstone 1858–64

Pacific explorers

Keeping time
Cook was the first explorer to take an accurate timepiece on a long voyage. Knowing the exact time enabled Cook to work out his longitude precisely, so Cook's maps and surveys were the most accurate of their era.

The Pacific is the world's largest ocean, but it was unknown to Europeans until Magellan's round-the-world voyage in the early 16th century. In the late 16th and early 17th centuries, Spanish sailors Álvaro de Mendaña and Fernández de Quirós sailed to the Solomon Islands, the Cook Islands and the New Hebrides. They hoped to find treasure, convert local people to Christianity and set up Spanish settlements. Meanwhile the Dutch East India Company, based in Batavia (Jakarta), was also exploring the area. Dutch sailors brought back stories of a vast and mysterious land to the south, 'Terra Australis Incognita' or Great Southern Continent.

The south Pacific

In the 18th century, British and French explorers searched the south Pacific for the Great Southern Continent. The man who finally solved the mystery was British seaman James Cook, who led three Pacific expeditions in the 1760s and 1770s. He first charted the two main islands of New Zealand and the whole of Australia's eastern coast, which would soon be settled by Europeans. He then sailed all the way round Antarctica, and thus proved that the fabled continent was a vast uninhabitable wilderness of rock and ice. Cook also discovered Hawaii on the way to find an entrance to the Northwest Passage from the Bering Sea, between Siberia and Alaska. Cook was famous for looking after his crew, insisting that they eat plenty of fresh fruit to prevent the sailor's disease of scurvy, which was common at the time.

Louis Bougainville
Bougainville was a French sailor who explored the Pacific at the same time as Cook. His voyage around the world took him to Tahiti, the Solomon Islands and the New Hebrides.

Cook and his team
Cook was one of the first scientific explorers. He took with him naturalists Joseph Banks and Daniel Solander to collect and record everything they discovered. The artist Sydney Parkinson painted many of the plants they found. In one place, they found so many new plants that Cook named the area Botany Bay.

Mapping Australia
The Dutch navigator Abel Tasman led two major Pacific expeditions between 1642 and 1643 on which he discovered Van Diemen's Land (Tasmania), and mapped large areas of the south-western Pacific and the Australian coastline for the Dutch East India Company.

Crossing Australia

Australia's first settlers lived near the coasts of the country's south-eastern corner. For years they did not go far inland, because the hot, dry climate made travel difficult, and the Blue Mountains cut off settlements such as Sydney from the interior. By the 1820s, explorers such as Charles Sturt were travelling along Australia's rivers, searching for new farmland. Soon after, Europeans including Edward Eyre, John Stuart and Robert O'Hara Burke pushed still further inland, to explore the mysteries of Australia's dry, unwelcoming interior.

John McDouall Stuart
John Stuart made several attempts to cross Australia. He finally reached the north coast, where he found a beach 'covered with a soft blue mud' in July 1862.

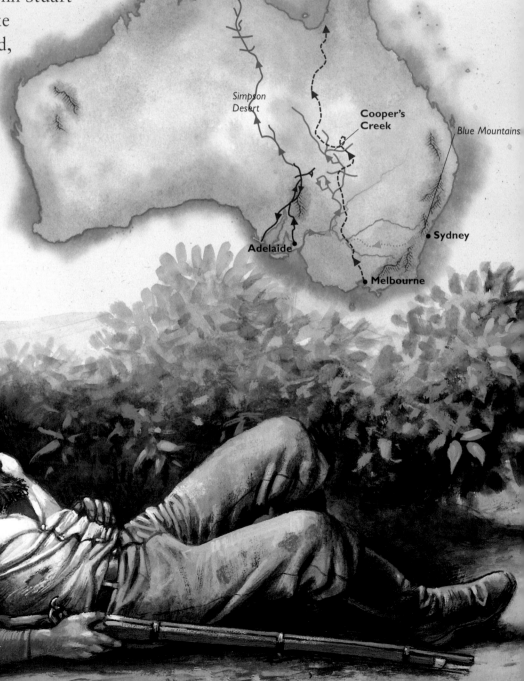

Exploring Australia

.... Sturt 1829–30

———— Eyre 1840

———— Sturt 1844–45

-------- Burke and Wills 1860–61

———— Stuart 1861 & 1862

Darwin

Simpson Desert

Cooper's Creek

Blue Mountains

Adelaide

Sydney

Melbourne

Routes across the desert

Several explorers tried to cross Australia from south to north, hoping to win a prize put up by the South Australian government. One of the first was Edward Eyre, who got stuck in the salt lakes and had to abandon his expedition. Charles Sturt got further, coming within 250km of Australia's parched centre. The first full crossing was by Robert O'Hara Burke and William Wills in 1860 to 1861. They used camels and set up camps along the way. Burke and Wills, with Charlie Gray and John King, made the full journey north, leaving the rest of their team at the Cooper's Creek camp. They hoped to meet up with the others on the way back.

Australian wildlife
Europeans were fascinated by Australia's unique wildlife. Creatures such as kangaroos were also a valuable source of meat for explorers in the bush.

Tragedy at Cooper's Creek
Gray died on the way, but Burke, Wills and King made it back to Cooper's Creek. However, the other team members had already left. Burke and Wills were exhausted and died of starvation at the empty camp. Only King lived to tell the tale.

The ends of the earth

By the end of the 19th century, the polar regions were still largely unexplored. Some ships had sailed quite near the North Pole and the Norwegian explorer Fridtjof Nansen got close in 1893 using sledges. An American team finally reached the North Pole itself in 1909. The South Pole, in the middle of the huge ice-bound continent of Antarctica, was a bigger challenge still. Glaciers, shelves of ice, howling winds and blinding snowstorms held explorers back. In 1908, the Irish explorer Ernest Shackleton led an expedition that got within 180km of the Pole. Then, in 1910, two expeditions, one led by Briton Robert Scott and the other by Norwegian Roald Amundsen, set off for the South Pole.

The _Fram_
Both Nansen and Amundsen sailed this ship. It was built with a reinforced hull so it would not be damaged if the ship froze into the ice.

The North Pole at last!
American explorer and naturalist Robert Peary wanted more than anything to reach the North Pole. It was on his eighth Arctic expedition, in April 1909, that Peary claimed to have reached the Pole. His expedition was well-prepared, and he had a large back-up team of Inuit, with many sledges and dogs. But people were suspicious; they thought that Peary could not have made the trip from his camp to the Pole and back to base in 16 days, as he claimed. However, recent investigations seem to support Peary's claim.

The race to the South Pole

Both Scott and Amundsen wanted to be the first to the South Pole. Scott had already led one expedition to Antarctica, when he discovered Edward VII Land. Amundsen was also very experienced, having sailed the Northwest Passage. Amundsen originally intended to sail to the Arctic in 1910, but changed his mind and went for the South Pole instead. The race was on. Both teams were well-prepared, but Scott insisted on using ponies to pull the sledges. When the ponies died, he and his men had to pull their sledges to the Pole. It was slow work. Scott described in his diary 'the soft snow clogging the skis and runners at every step, the sledge groaning'. Amundsen used dogs, and was quicker. As a result, Amundsen won the race, on 14 December 1911. Scott arrived on 17 January 1912. He and all his men perished on the way back to their base.

Scott at Cape Evans
The British explorer set up a comfortable winter base at Cape Evans for his men. At his desk, Scott wrote a detailed diary and studied the results of the expedition's scientific work. Scott took several scientists with him, and they did important work recording weather patterns, collecting rock samples and observing glaciers. They also studied Antarctica's most famous bird, the emperor penguin.

Dog power
Amundsen and his team travelled on sledges pulled by dogs, just as the Inuit did. The dogs served them well. For much of the journey they covered over 20km per day, which is good going in the fierce icy wind of Antarctica. Amundsen looked after his dogs, but he had to be ruthless. When they were near the South Pole, there were too many dogs to be fed properly, and he ordered some of the animals to be killed.

EXPLORATION AND SCIENCE

Unlike previous explorers, most of whom voyaged to found settlements or to make their fortunes through trade, many 19th- and 20th-century explorers travelled for science – to observe new species of plants and animals, and examine rocks and fossils. Scientists on an expedition search for new knowledge and record everything they find. One of the most famous was naturalist Charles Darwin, whose travels inspired and provided evidence for his theory of evolution. More recent explorers, such as those who dive into deep ocean trenches, make fascinating discoveries about life on our planet and the way different ecosystems work. Science, through new technologies and inventions, also helps exploration and makes it safer. Whether they are using digital cameras, satellite navigation equipment or the latest tough, lightweight climbing boots, explorers take advantage of the best that scientists and inventors can provide.

Core of the problem
Understanding climate change can help us plan for the future. Antarctic scientists explore past variations in the weather by drilling ice cores – long columns of ice from deep below the surface. The ice contains particles of dust and chemicals that can show how the climate has changed over hundreds, even thousands, of years.

The _Kon-Tiki_
Norwegian archaeologist Thor Heyerdahl was fascinated
by the similarities between the ancient cultures of South
America and those of the Pacific islands. He wondered
whether the people from Peru could have travelled to the
South Seas. To test this theory, Heyerdahl built a balsa-wood
raft, the _Kon-Tiki_, and sailed it 6,900km from Peru to Polynesia
in 1947. He showed that ancient navigators could have made
the journey using the technology of ancient times.

In pursuit of knowledge

In the 18th and 19th centuries, naturalists travelled to many parts of the world, such as South America, Africa and Southeast Asia, that were little-known to Europeans. They were amazed by the dense forests and vast rivers, and by the incredible variety of plants and animals. Richest of all were the tropical forests of South America, which played host to many explorers. German Alexander von Humboldt and Frenchman Aimé Bonpland travelled through the Andes Mountains. British naturalists Alfred Russel Wallace and Henry Bates explored the Amazon Basin. The most famous of the naturalists was Briton Charles Darwin.

Darwin's finches
Darwin observed several different species of finches on the Galapagos Islands. The birds had evolved different beaks to eat the foods available on different islands. So the finches of one island developed thin beaks to spear bark-dwelling insects, while those on other islands evolved broad beaks to crack open shellfish. The birds helped prove Darwin's theory of evolution.

Darwin at work
Charles Darwin was uncomfortable aboard ship. His quarters were cramped and he suffered from seasickness. Even so, he managed to fill many notebooks with his observations.

Humboldt in Ecuador
The German naturalist admires a volcano near Quito, Ecuador. In 1802, Humboldt climbed another volcano, Mount Chimborazo, reaching 5,800m, a world record climb at the time.

Plant life
Bonpland drew thousands of plants, such as this *Inga excelsa*, which were unknown in Europe. Many of his drawings were published in Humboldt's huge 23-volume book about their travels.

Darwin and the *Beagle*

Darwin was only 23 years old in 1831 when he was given the job of scientist aboard the *Beagle*. The ship sailed all the way around the world, but Darwin's most important work was done in South America and on the Galapagos Islands. Darwin was excited by what he found, especially in the rainforests. He discovered thousands of species and used his research to write his groundbreaking book on evolution, *On the Origin of Species*. In the Brazilian jungle, Darwin was amazed by the noise of millions of insects, which was 'so loud that it may be heard even in a vessel anchored several hundred yards from the shore'.

The route of the *Beagle*
The *Beagle* spent over three years of its voyage in the waters around South America before crossing the Pacific, Indian and Atlantic oceans back to Britain.

Scaling the peaks

People have been fascinated by the height and grandeur of mountain peaks for thousands of years, but climbing as a sport only began in the 18th century. The first mountaineers explored the European Alps and by about 1870, they had scaled all the highest peaks in Europe. Since then, climbers have travelled all over the world, mapping the world's greatest peaks. New equipment and a greater understanding of the effects of altitude on the human body meant that, by the 1960s, the world's highest peaks above 8,000m had been climbed.

Boots from Hillary's expedition
These leather boots from the 1950s were specially made for the Everest expedition. They were designed to be light and keep in heat. Each boot had two layers of leather, with opossum fur between the layers for warmth.

Conquering Everest
On Sir John Hunt's 1953 expedition, New Zealand climber Edmund Hillary and Tenzin Norgay of Nepal were the first to climb to the top of Everest, at 8,848m the world's highest peak. Their team used a camp at about 4,000m to acclimatize themselves to the lack of oxygen. As they climbed, they rested regularly to recover from the effects of the altitude.

Europe's highest mountain

In 1760, Horace-Bénédict de Saussure, from Geneva, offered a prize for the first mountaineer to climb Mont Blanc in the Alps, the highest mountain in Europe. Frenchman Michel-Gabriel Paccard claimed the prize money in 1786. Saussure climbed the peak the following year. He used ladders on the difficult descent.

Modern climbing boots

These boots are made from artificial fibres and plastic, and are lightweight, warm and waterproof. The materials also dry very quickly, which is important in icy temperatures when wet boots can freeze solid.

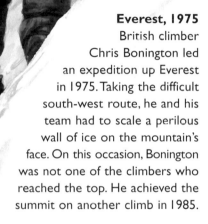

Everest, 1975

British climber Chris Bonington led an expedition up Everest in 1975. Taking the difficult south-west route, he and his team had to scale a perilous wall of ice on the mountain's face. On this occasion, Bonington was not one of the climbers who reached the top. He achieved the summit on another climb in 1985.

Knowledge as a lifeline

Mountaineers need to be able to cope with high winds, steep rock faces and, worst of all, a lack of oxygen at altitude. The latest scientific knowledge and equipment have always helped. By the 1920s, doctors had discovered that climbers needed to spend time getting used to high-altitude conditions in order to survive at still higher levels without getting sick. By the time of the successful British Everest expedition in 1953, climbers had discovered that an extra oxygen supply at extreme altitudes improved their performance. They used the latest breathing apparatus, even though this was heavy and a burden to carry. Sir John Hunt, the expedition leader, said: 'But for oxygen, we should certainly not have got to the top'.

Finding the *Titanic*
The British luxury liner the *Titanic* sank off Newfoundland after striking an iceberg in 1912 – about 1,500 people drowned. The wreck lay undisturbed at the bottom of the sea until found by a salvage team led by the American Robert Ballard in 1985. The team later used a manned submersible called the *Alvin*, together with a small remote-controlled vehicle, to film and photograph the wreck.

The ocean depths

Over two-thirds of the earth's surface is covered with water, but the ocean depths remain the least explored parts of the globe. This is because the sea is a dangerous place. To stay underwater for any length of time, people need breathing apparatus. For deep dives, we need special equipment to protect us from the crushing pressure of the water. Because of this, scientists have only recently been able to study deep oceans. But the things divers have found, from bizarre deep-sea creatures to intriguing shipwrecks, have fascinated people all over the world.

Aqualung

In 1943, French scientist and film-maker Jacques Cousteau invented the aqualung (or scuba lung), a portable breathing apparatus which allowed him to dive without a link to the surface. Cousteau made dives all over the world using the aqualung, filming the stunning wildlife he saw. His device is now used by divers worldwide.

Deeper and deeper

Ocean explorers made deeper and deeper dives during the 20th century, but in the deepest ocean trenches the pressure was too great even for craft like the bathysphere. The breakthrough came in 1953, when Auguste Piccard, a Belgian inventor and diver, revealed his bathyscaphe, or deep-water vessel, the *Trieste*. In 1960, Piccard's son Jacques and American naval officer Don Walsh made the ultimate dive in the *Trieste II* – 10,924m to the bottom of the world's deepest trench, the Marianas Trench in the Pacific. Those on board found a whole new world of remarkable deep-sea animals.

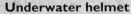

Beebe's bathysphere

The reinforced steel bathysphere ('deep ball') was designed by American diver Charles William Beebe in the 1930s. Its strong walls protected Beebe from the high pressure of the water as he dived to depths of over 900m off Bermuda.

Underwater helmet

Divers in the 19th century wore heavy metal helmets such as this one, designed by German inventor Augustus Siebe. A long tube linked the helmet to the surface, and air was pumped down the tube, to enable the diver to breathe. When the diver breathed out, the used air bubbled out through a pipe beneath the neck.

Maps and mapping

Today, we take maps for granted, but modern maps would not exist without the work of the explorers and surveyors who travelled into unknown territory and recorded the lie of the land. Ancient maps were not usually very accurate. There were a lot of unknown areas, and map-makers often resorted to guesswork to fill in the gaps. But as exploration increased and surveying techniques improved, maps became clearer, more accurate and easier to use.

Dividers
Simple metal dividers have been used for centuries to measure distances on maps. By lining up the ends of the two arms with two points on the map, then moving them to the map's scale bar, the user can easily measure the distance between two places.

Ptolemy's world
Maps of the late 15th century were still based mainly on the *Geographia*, a book by the Egyptian-born Greek scholar Ptolemy written in the 2nd century CE. He described the world of the ancient Greeks and Romans – Europe, West Asia and North Africa. Almost everything else was 'Terra incognita', unknown land.

The Renaissance world

By the 16th century, the Renaissance, or revival of scholarship, had combined with the work of European explorers to improve world maps. This map benefits from the knowledge of Central and North America brought back by explorers such as Columbus, from information about Africa provided by the Portuguese navigators, and from data brought back by round-the-world sailors including Drake and del Cano. Even so, there are huge gaps – little was known about South America, and the map-maker has guessed the size of the legendary Great Southern Continent.

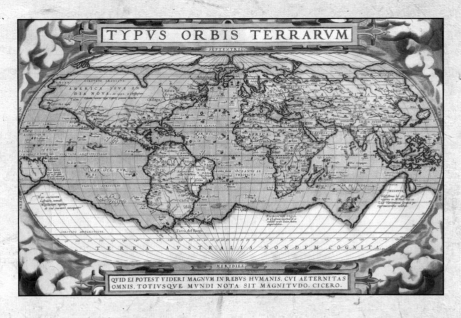

The story of map-making

Before 1600, most European world maps looked the same – they were based on the Mediterranean and often had Jerusalem at the centre. But, gradually, maps improved as explorers discovered more details of Africa, Asia, the Americas and finally Australia. The growth of the printing industry in the 16th century also made maps easier to come by – before, each map had to be drawn by hand. In the 18th century, surveying became more organized. The first national survey began in France and surveyors travelled west with the new immigrants to North America, mapping land available for settlement. By the 19th century, surveys set new standards of accuracy. Some, such as the British Ordnance Survey (which began publishing maps in 1801) and the US Geological Survey (begun in 1879) provided the ancestors of today's maps.

The 17th-century world

By the late 17th century, the Dutch had sent their explorers into the southern Indian Ocean. Map-makers were therefore able to chart large parts of Australia's coast, although they still thought it was part of a huge southern continent. On this map, the map-maker has avoided guesswork, hence the gaps in the Australian coast.

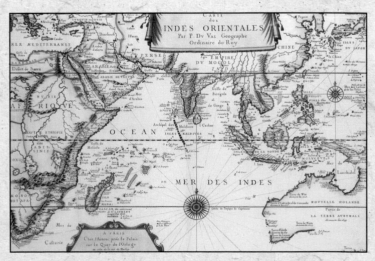

Sextant

The sextant, invented in the 18th century, was used by explorers and surveyors to work out their latitude. The user looked through the sight and adjusted a moving bar until the sun seemed to line up with the horizon. A latitude measurement could then be read on the curving scale at the bottom of the sextant.

Nowadays, the information used to put together a map can come from several different sources. A map-maker may arrange for a special survey to be made that measures distances and height on the ground, and builds up accurate drawings from the results. Aerial photographs, taken from an aircraft with a camera pointing vertically down towards the ground, provide another source of information. In addition, many of the satellites that orbit the earth send signals from which scientists can build up detailed pictures of the terrain.

Map-making decisions

There are many different types of maps – sea charts, town plans, territorial maps and maps showing the features of the countryside – and a map-maker has to decide what type is needed before starting work. One of the main ways in which maps vary is in their scale – the relative size at which the features are shown. Small-scale maps do not show much detail, but can include a large area, so a small scale is useful for maps of entire countries or even the world. Larger scales give more detail and so are used to show smaller areas. Many features are shown as symbols on maps – they can range from special marks to represent towns or buildings to coloured shading for land at different heights above sea-level. Maps also have a grid – the straight lines that help us work out where we are on the map. These are often based on the lines of latitude and longitude that circle the earth.

In the round

Globes are maps in three dimensions. A globe has one big advantage – if it is drawn correctly, all distances, areas and heights can be in almost exactly the right proportions as the earth. This is impossible on a two-dimensional map.

Map projections

A projection is a way of depicting all or part of the three-dimensional globe on a two-dimensional map. There are many ways of doing this, and they produce quite different results. Some projections, such as the one (right) devised by the 16th-century Dutch map-maker Mercator, depicts all the compass bearings accurately, and so is ideal for navigators. Others, such as the zenithal projection (below right), show the surface areas of the earth's landmasses in proportion and are used to calculate surface area, such as for maps showing land-use.

Flying high

Satellites carrying instruments that can detect the features on the planet below using infrared waves produce detailed images that can be beamed back to earth. These images can show many types of items on the planet's surface – from buildings and vegetation to various types of rocks – and can then be used by a map-maker.

Timeline

1492BCE
Queen Hatshepsut of Egypt sends an expedition to the land of Punt.

470BCE
Phoenician sailor Hanno explores Africa's north and west coasts.

c. 330BCE
Pytheas, an explorer from Greece, sails to the northern land of Thule.

138BCE
Chang Ch'ien of China begins his long journey by land across Asia.

CE629–645
Buddhist monk Hsüan Tsang travels west from China and explores India.

C. CE1000
Viking seafarer Leif Eriksson arrives in Newfoundland.

CE1260
The Polo brothers, Maffeo and Niccolo, merchants from Venice, set off on a journey that takes them all the way to the Chinese capital Cambaluc (Beijing).

CE1352
Muslim traveller Ibn Battuta sets off on his journey across the Sahara Desert.

CE1485–86
Diogo Cão of Portugal sails to Cape Cross on the Namibian coast.

CE1487–88
Bartolomeu Dias becomes the first Portuguese navigator to sail around the Cape of Good Hope and reach the Indian Ocean.

CE1492–93
Italian Christopher Columbus makes his first of four voyages across the Atlantic.

CE1497
John Cabot sails from Bristol, England, across the Atlantic Ocean. He reaches Newfoundland before turning back.

CE1497–98
Vasco da Gama of Portugal sails along the African coast and across the Indian Ocean to India.

CE1519
Portuguese sailor Ferdinand Magellan begins his round-the-world voyage. He dies, but one ship makes it back to Spain in 1522, under Juan Sebastián del Cano.

CE1519–21
Spaniard Hernan Cortés sails to and conquers Mexico.

CE1531–33
Francisco Pizarro conquers the Inca empire of Peru for Spain.

CE1535–38
French sea-captain Jacques Cartier explores Canada's St Lawrence River.

CE1539–42
Hernando de Soto from Spain conquers Florida and explores the Mississippi River in North America.

CE1576
English navigator Martin Frobisher sails to Baffin Island in search of the Northwest Passage. He trades with Inuits and returns home.

CE1577–80
Englishman Francis Drake sails around the world.

CE1594–97
Dutchman Willem Barents leads three voyages to find the Northeast Passage.

CE1603
French fur trader Samuel de Champlain arrives in North America. He becomes the founder of French Canada.

CE1610–11
Searching for the Northwest Passage, Englishman Henry Hudson reaches Hudson Bay before dying in its icy waters.

CE1642–43
Dutchman Abel Tasman explores the Pacific, and makes the European discovery of Van Diemen's Land, New Zealand and Fiji.

CE1669–80
Robert Cavelier de la Salle, a French fur trader, explores Canada's Great Lakes.

CE1690
Briton Edmund Halley invents the diving bell for underwater exploration.

CE1766–69
Frenchman Louis Bougainville sails around the world and across the Pacific, visiting the Solomon Islands and the New Hebrides. The Great Barrier Reef prevents him from reaching Australia.

CE1768–71
The British Navy sends James Cook on the first of his Pacific voyages of scientific discovery. He sails around New Zealand and navigates Australia's eastern coast, collecting many scientific specimens.

CE1796
Scotsman Mungo Park explores the Niger River. He drowned on his second expedition in 1805.

CE1799–1804
German scientist Humboldt and French naturalist Bonpland travel in South America making many important scientific discoveries.

CE1803
US President Thomas Jefferson chooses Meriwether Lewis and William Clark to explore Louisiana, the territory that the USA had purchased from France.

CE1828
Frenchman René Caillié, disguised in local Arab dress, visits the great trading city of Timbuktu in the Sahara Desert.

CE1828–30
Charles Sturt explores rivers in south-eastern Australia, such as the Macquarie.

CE1831–36
Charles Darwin, British naturalist on the round-the-world voyage of the *Beagle*, visits South America and the Galapagos Islands. What he saw helped him form his theory of evolution.

CE1840–41
Edward John Eyre journeys from Adelaide to Albany along Australia's southern coast.

CE1844–46
Charles Sturt travels towards the centre of Australia, proving that there is a desert at the heart of the continent.

CE1845–47
John Franklin sails far to the west of Baffin Island before perishing after his ship is trapped in the ice for 18 months.

CE1848–52
Britons Alfred Russel Wallace and Henry Walter Bates explore the Amazon Basin.

CE1850–55
German Heinrich Barth crosses the Sahara Desert from Tripoli to Kano.

CE1857
Briton John Hanning Speke begins a series of expeditions in East Africa, which lead to the discovery of Lake Victoria and the source of the Nile.

CE1860–61
Robert O'Hara Burke and William Wills make the land crossing from Australia's south to north coast.

CE1871
Scotsman David Livingstone, on his fourth journey across southern Africa, is thought to be lost, but is found by American Henry Morton Stanley.

CE1872–76
The oceanographic exploration ship *HMS Challenger* undertakes a long voyage around the world. Scientists on board study every ocean except the Arctic.

CE1878–79
Swedish explorer Nils Nordenskjöld sails through the Northeast Passage.

CE1893–96
Norwegian Fridtjof Nansen sails across the Arctic Ocean in the *Fram* and then sets off towards the North Pole on foot. He does not reach the Pole, but gets closer than anyone has before.

CE1903–06
Norwegian Roald Amundsen is the first person to sail the Northwest Passage.

CE1908–09
Americans Robert Peary and Matthew Henson claim to reach the North Pole.

CE1910–12
Roald Amundsen leads the first expedition to reach the South Pole.

CE1910–12
Briton Robert Falcon Scott leads an expedition to Antarctica. Scott and his colleagues die on their return journey from the South Pole.

CE1914–16
Irishman Ernest Shackleton tries to cross Antarctica from the Weddell Sea to the Ross Sea. He has to abandon ship.

CE1934
American inventor Charles Beebe makes a record-breaking dive in his bathysphere.

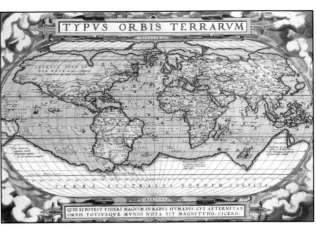

CE1943
French scientist Jacques Cousteau invents the aqualung, which makes underwater exploration easier and safer.

CE1960
Frenchman Jacques Piccard descends nearly 11,000m into the Marianas Trench in the Pacific, in the bathyscaphe *Trieste*.

CE1979–82
The Transglobe Expedition, led by Briton Ranulph Fiennes, follows the meridian around the earth, crossing both poles.

CE1993
Ranulph Fiennes and Dr Michael Stroud make the first unsupported crossing of Antarctica on foot – 2,172km in 88 days.

CE1999
Swiss pilot Bertrand Piccard and Briton Brian Jones are the first to fly a balloon, the *Breitling Orbiter*, non-stop around the world, climbing 11,000m above the earth.

CE2001
American Ann Bancroft and Norwegian Liv Arnesen become the first women to cross Antarctica on skis.

Glossary

acclimatize To get used to a new climate or habitat.

allies People or countries who join in an alliance for mutual benefit.

altitude Height, usually above sea-level.

analyze To carefully study the different parts of something.

archaeologist A person who studies the remains and monuments of ancient times.

barren Land that has no or hardly any vegetation growing on it.

bathysphere A round, deep-sea diving vessel, lowered underwater by a cable.

bearing The direction of a place measured from a fixed point.

blizzards Storms in which heavy snow is combined with a strong, cold wind.

botany The scientific study of plants.

bow The front of a ship.

bush Unsettled or uncultivated area of land, covered with shrubs or trees.

caravan A number of travellers or traders travelling together over land.

cocoons The silky cases spun by insects such as silk worms that protect them during the period when they change into an adult.

colonies Settlements set up at some distance from, but usually still governed by, the people's original homeland.

conquistadores Spanish conquerors of Central and South America in the 15th and 16th centuries.

continent One of the seven large landmasses of the world – Asia, Africa, Europe, Oceania, North America, South America and Antarctica.

creek A stream or small river.

crevasses Deep cracks in the ice of a glacier.

ecosystem An entire environment, comprising an area, the living and non-living things that inhabit it, and the interactions between them.

environment All the external surroundings in which a plant, animal or human being lives; everything that affects its growth and well-being.

equator The imaginary line around the earth, halfway between the poles.

evolution The development of a living or non-living thing. Darwin's theory of evolution shows how all animals have evolved over millions of years to be as they are today.

gilded Something that is covered with gold or a gold-like substance.

glaciers Rivers of ice that move very slowly down mountain slopes.

Global Positioning System (GPS) A navigation system that enables people to locate their position accurately by using radio signals from satellites.

globe The earth, or a map of the earth printed onto a ball.

gondola In air travel, the capsule or container hanging beneath a balloon or airship, carrying cargo or passengers.

habitat The natural home of a plant or animal, such as a desert, rainforest, ocean or town.

headland An area of land that sticks out into the sea – a cape is a headland.

humid Moist or damp – used especially of climate or the moisture content of the air.

hydrogen A very light, colourless, flammable gas, which is sometimes used to fill balloons and was formerly used in airships.

import To bring goods into a country from abroad.

infrared waves Invisible waves of light that radiate out from the earth's surface that can be used to monitor various geographical features from space.

jungle Forest in the tropical regions or near the equator, with dense growth of plants and trees.

latitude Distance north or south of the equator, measured in degrees.

longitude Distance east or west of the prime meridian, measured in degrees.

malaria Infectious disease spread by the bite of a certain type of mosquito, which causes recurring chills and fevers.

merchants People who buy and sell goods in large quantities.

meridian An imaginary line around the earth through both poles. Lines of longitude are measured east and west of the prime meridian, which runs through Greenwich, London, UK.

missionaries People who travel on behalf of a church, or other religious body, to preach and perform community service.

native Belonging to a country.

naturalists Scientists who study animals, plants, or other aspects of the natural world.

orbit The path that a satellite or similar body follows as it circles a planet.

parasails Parachute-like sails used to pull people on skis over the snow.

pioneers People who are the first to do something, such as the explorers who travelled into uncharted land of North America to found colonies.

polar At or near either of the earth's poles; more loosely, in the Arctic or Antarctic regions of the earth.

portolan chart A type of sea map used by early explorers on which compass bearings are shown as straight lines radiating from a number of points.

pressure The pushing force exerted by one body or substance on another.

rainforest Forest or jungle found in tropical areas; its typical features are dense vegetation and heavy rainfall.

skidoos Vehicles used for travelling across snow; also known as snowmobiles.

specimens Items, such as plants, animals or pieces of rock, collected by an explorer to show the typical features of an area or habitat.

stern The rear part of a ship.

strait A narrow channel of water linking two oceans or seas.

submersible An underwater vessel, such as a small submarine, that can work in waters too deep for divers.

survey To measure and work out distances and heights in an area, and produce a map.

terrain An area of ground.

territory Land; an area of land owned by a country.

treaty A legal agreement between two countries or states.

trench A deep ditch or valley sometimes on the ocean floor, such as the Marianas Trench.

tropical In the tropics, the region of the earth marked by two lines of latitude – the Tropic of Cancer and the Tropic of Capricorn.

vegetation Plant growth.

ventilation The way of allowing fresh air into an area. Ventilated clothes allow excess heat to escape, keeping an explorer at a comfortable temperature.

navigate To travel by ship or boat, or to plan the course of a journey.

navigator Person who navigates a ship; someone skilled in navigation.

New World The name given to the Americas by Europeans in the 15th century, when explorers discovered the vast, previously unknown landmass.

nomadic Lifestyle that involves moving from place to place to find land and food.

runners Strips of metal or wood on which a sledge runs.

satellites Objects that orbit the earth or another planet.

scholars Educated people.

scurvy Disease, caused by lack of vitamin C, that makes the sufferer bleed beneath the skin.

secondary jungle Plant growth in a jungle that regrows after part of the forest has been cleared; its typical feature is very thick plant growth near the forest floor.

Index

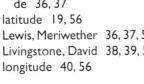

Acknowledgements

The publishers would like to thank the following illustrators for their contributions to this book:
b = bottom, *c* = centre, *l* = left, *t* = top, *m* = middle
Nigel Chamberlain *cover left*, 50–51; **Gino D'Achille** 44–45; **Douglas Harken** 49 *br*; **Gary Hinks** 49 *bc*; **Adam Hook** 12–13, 58 *tl*; **Richard Hook** 18–19, 28–29; **John James** 37 *tr* ; **Jack Keay** 22 *cl*; **Linden Artists Ltd** 12 *bl*; **Kevin Maddison** 16 *tc*, 16 *tr*; **Salariya/Willii** 17 *tl*; **Mike Sanders** 37 *t*, 39 *b*, 42 *c*; **Claudia Saraceni** 43 *tr*; **Thomas Trojer** 10 *tl*; **Richard Ward** 12 *tl*; **Mike White** *cover right*, 8–9, 14–15, 24–25, 30–31, 32–33, 36–37, 40–41, 42–43, 46–47, 48–49; **Paul Wright** 34–35, 38–39.

The publishers would like to thank the following for supplying photographs for this book:
b = bottom, *c* = centre, *l* = left, *t* = top, *m* = middle
Pages: **4** *bl* Corbis; **5** *t* Royal Geographical Society/J.T. Studley; **5** *cl* The Royal Geographical Society/Brunei Rainforest Project 91–92/Chris Coldicott; **6** *tl* The Royal Geographical Society; **6** *cr* Raleigh International; **6** *bl* The Royal Geographical Society; **7** *cr* The Royal Geographical Society; **10** *bl* Werner Forman Archive; **13** *tr* Ancient Art & Architecture Collection/R. Sheridan; **15** *tr* The Royal Geographical Society/Ian MacWilliam; **15** *cl* Corbis; **15** *br* Ancient Art & Architecture Collection/R. Sheridan; **17** *cr* Werner Forman Archive/National Museum, Copenhagen; **19** *tr* The Bridgeman Art Library/Topkapi Palace Museum, Istanbul, Turkey; **19** *cr* Bruce Coleman Collection/Joe McDonald; **21** *tr* The Bridgeman Art Library/British Library, London, UK; **22** *tl* The Art Archive/Golestan Palace, Teheran/Dagli Orti; **22–23** *b* The Art Archive/Bibliothéque Nationale, Paris; **23** *tl* The Master and Fellows of Corpus Christi College, Cambridge; **24** *tr* Art Directors & Trip Photographic Library/A. Tovy; **25** *cr* The Art Archive/Naval Museum, Genoa/Dagli Orti; **26** *tl* The Bridgeman Art Library; **26** *cr* Corbis; **26** *bl* The Bridgeman Art Library/Library of Congress, Washington D.C., USA; **28** *tr* The Bridgeman Art Library; **29** *tr* The Bridgeman Art Library/Victoria & Albert Museum, London; **31** *tl* British Library 10460.ee.15; **31** *tr* National Maritime Museum Picture Library; **31** *cr* The Art Archive; **33** *c* yourexpedition.com; **34** *bl* AKG London; **37** *cr* The Bridgeman Art Library/Brooklyn Museum of Art, New York, USA; **37** *bl* AKG London; **38** *bl* The Art Archive/Musée des Arts Africains et Océaniens/Dagli Orti; **39** *tr* The Royal Geographical Society; **39** *cr* Science & Society Photo Library/National Museum of Photography, Film & TV; **40** *tl* National Maritime Museum Picture Library; **41** *tr* AKG London; **41** *cr* The Art Archive; **42** *tr* The Art Archive; **44** *bl* Corbis; **45** *tr* Corbis; **46** *cl* Science Photo Library; **49** *tl* The Art Archive/Navy Historical Service, Vincennes, France/Dagli Orti; **49** *tr* The Natural History Museum, London; **50** *cr* The Royal Geographical Society/Alfred Gregory; **51** *tl* The Art Archive/University Library, Geneva/Dagli Orti; **51** *cl* Chris Bonington Picture Library; **53** *tl* BBC Natural History Unit Picture Library; **53** *cr* Corbis; **53** *bc* Science Photo Library; **54** *tl* Science Photo Library; **54–55** *c* Science & Society Picture Library; **56** *tl* The Art Archive/South Australia Art Gallery; **56** *br* The Bridgeman Art Library; **57** *cl* Science Photo Library/GE Astro Space.

*Every effort has been made to trace the copyright holders of the photographs.
The publishers apologise for any inconvenience caused.*

Below is a list of useful websites:
www.rgs.org (The Royal Geographical Society)
www.raleigh.org.uk (Raleigh International, UK)
www.explorers.org (The Explorers Club)
www.nationalgeographic.com (National Geographic)
www.ses-explore.org (Scientific Exploration Society)